D1381211

POCKET GRACES

POCKET GRACES

COMPILED BY
PAM ROBERTSON

CHURCH HOUSE
PUBLISHING

Church House Publishing
Church House
Great Smith Street
London SW1P 3NZ
Tel: 020 7898 1451
Fax: 020 7898 1449

ISBN 0 7151 4042 6

Published 1994 by The National Society and
Church House Publishing

Typeset by Vitaset, Paddock Wood, Kent
Printed in England by the University Printing House,
Cambridge

Contents

TO MY HUSBAND VIC
IN GRATITUDE FOR HIS LOVE, PATIENCE
AND AFFIRMATION OVER THE YEARS

*Taking the five loaves and the two fish
and looking up to heaven, he gave thanks
and broke the loaves. Then he gave them
to the disciples, and the disciples gave
them to the people.*

Matthew 14.19

GENERAL GRACES

For what we are about to receive
May the Lord make us truly thankful.

We break the bread of brotherhood,
And thank thee, Lord, for all things good.
May we, more blessed than we deserve,
Live less for self, and more to serve. Amen.

God, we thank you for this food,
For rest and home and all things good,
For wind and rain and sun above,
But most of all for those we love.

May God bless this food to our use
And ourselves in his service.
For Jesus' sake. Amen.

✳

For good food, good friends and
    good fellowship,
We thank you, Lord, in Jesus' name.

✳

Father, as your gospel teaches,
We must love in word and deed.
Bless us gathered round this table
Help us share with those in need.

✳

For food and friendship day by day,
we bless you, heavenly father.

Lord, for these and all your gifts,
    we give you thanks.
In thanks to God for all his benefits
Let us have a moment's silence for the
    hungry of the world.

Bless those that sit at this table, the food
that is on it, and those who prepared it.
Amen.

Pam Robertson

As we gather in this place,
Brief but heartfelt is our grace:
Thank you, Lord, for friends and food.
Thank you, Lord, for all things good.

Audrey Stanley

O Lord Jesus, Bread of life,
bless this food that it may bring
refreshment to our bodies
and healing to our souls now and for ever.

We have food while others are starving.
We have companions while others
    are alone.
May the goodness we receive
    strengthen our resolve
    to share your blessings
    with all your children.

David W. Lankshear

For these gifts of food and your care
    day by day,
heavenly father, we thank you. Amen.

F. W. Street

In giving you thanks for this food, we give
you thanks for all those who have worked
so that we may enjoy it.

Heavenly Father,
We thank you for our homes and families,
for our food and clothing, and for all the
happiness that parents and children can
share. We ask that your love may surround
us, your care protect us and that we may
know your peace at all times,
for Jesus' sake. Amen.

M. H. Botting

Father, we thank thee for the night,
And for the pleasant morning light;
For rest and food and loving care,
And all that makes the day so fair.

Help us to do the things we should,
To be to others kind and good;
In all we do at work or play,
To grow more loving every day.

Rebecca J. Weston (c.1890)

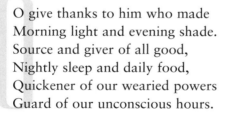

O give thanks to him who made
Morning light and evening shade.
Source and giver of all good,
Nightly sleep and daily food,
Quickener of our wearied powers
Guard of our unconscious hours.

Josiah Condor (1836)

Gracious God, may the food that we are
about to receive strengthen our bodies, and
may thy Holy Spirit strengthen and refresh
our souls through Jesus Christ.

The Tent and the Altar

Lord God, we thank you for all the good
things of your providing, and we pray for
the time when people everywhere shall have
the abundant life of your will, revealed to
us in Jesus Christ your Son, our Lord.

Bishop George Appleton (1902–93)

God, you give good things liberally and
judge not. May all who shall eat and drink
together at this table be joined in true
friendship, and praise you with thankful
hearts: through Jesus Christ our Lord.

May God relieve the wants of others and
give us thankful hearts: for Christ's sake.

John Dallas

✳

O Lord, give us grateful hearts
For the food now set before us
And supply the wants of others.
For Christ's sake.

Charles Shepherd

✳

Lord, make us thankful, for this food
and for all your love,
through Jesus Christ our Lord.

✳

O you who clothe the lilies
and feed the birds of the air
Who lead the lambs to pasture
and the hart to the water's side.

Who has multiplied loaves and fishes
and converted water into wine,
Come to our table
as giver and guest to dine.

Stephen Doyle OFM

For food to eat, and those who prepare it,
For health to enjoy it, and friends to share it,
We thank thee, O Lord.

Charles Shepherd

O Heavenly Father, who by thy blessed Son
has taught us to ask of thee our daily bread:
Have compassion on the millions of our
fellow men who live in poverty and hunger;
relieve their distress, make plain the way of
help and grant thy grace unto us all,
that we may bear each other's burdens
according to thy will,
through Jesus Christ our Lord.

Bishop George Appleton (1902-93)

For all the glory of the way.
For thy protection night and day.
For roof-tree, fire, and bed and board
For all thy gifts we thank you, Lord.

The Wayfarers' Grace
M. Elizabeth Worsfold

O God, we thank you for the gift of life
and for the faculties which enable us to
enjoy it. You have given us our eyes to see
the beauty of the world, our ears to hear
speech and the sound of music, our
tongues to taste the good food of your
creation, our lips with which to speak in
friendship to others and our hands with
which to minister to their needs. Help us
through the grace of your Holy Spirit,
to use all that we have in your service
and for your greater glory.
Through Jesus Christ our Lord.

Blessed are you, Lord our God, king of the
universe who feeds the entire world in his
goodness, with grace, with kindness and
with mercy. He gives food to all for his
kindness is eternal. Blessed are you, God,
who nourishes all.

Blessed art thou, O Lord our God, king of
the universe, who bringest forth bread
from the earth.

GRACES FOR ORGANIZATIONS

The Army

Thank you, Lord, for this Mess. Amen.

For good fellowship in freedom,
And for those who made it possible,
We give thanks.

Cecil Hunt

The Navy

No chaplain. Thank God. Amen.

Lord, I've got it down.
You keep it down.

Grace on board ship

God save the King,
Bless our dinners,
Make us thankful.

Admiral Lord Nelson (1758–1805)

The Air Force

For the spirit of adventure which takes
    us into the air,
For the grace of God which brings us
    safely back to earth,
For the comradeship which draws
    us together,
For the blessing of good food,
For these and all his mercies
    God's holy name be praised. Amen

Group Captain E. F. Haylock, RAF (Retd)

War veterans

For valour – a phrase so short
and yet a world of meaning caught
and held for all to learn.

In muddy trench and foreign field
where terror cried, 'it's hopeless, yield!'
quiet hope and courage burned.

In flaming aircraft, sinking wreck,
smoking cockpit, bloodstained deck,
brave hearts and spirits turned.

'Thank God for valour' be our grace.
'For friends in this and every place,
for food and freedom dearly earned.'

A grace for gatherings of service veterans, originally written
for a lunch for 50 VCs held at the Royal Tournament

Patrick Forbes

Bankers

Father, for money, for pfennigs and francs,
for deutschmarks and sterling
we yield you our thanks.
When equities soar and bulls prowl around
Keep us from greed and our feet on
    the ground.

Architects and surveyors

Lord God, survey us with serenity, measure
us with mercy and build us through this
feast into a people fit to please you (and
our clients) now and for ever.

Christopher Herbert

Estate agents

Dear God, architect of the universe, bless
this food to our use and grant us through
its nourishment to have a gift with words,
an eye for a south-facing aspect and the
confidence and humility to meet our clients'
every need, now and always. Amen.

Christopher Herbert

✳

The Women's Institute

Thank God for dirty dishes,
They have a tale to tell.
Whilst other folk go hungry
We've eaten very well.
For home and health, and happiness
We shouldn't make a fuss,
For by this pile of evidence,
God's been very good to us.

✳

The Rotary Club

O Lord and giver of all good,
We thank thee for our daily food,
May Rotary aims and Rotary ways
Help us to serve thee all our days.

＊

Cricketers

O Lord, you'd scarcely think it wicket
to give you thanks for wondrous cricket,
to celebrate the fans who make
and send those lovely gifts of cake.
Now shades of that great Grace attend
to take guard at the gasworks end
and praise with us the life of Brian
whose commentaries we all rely on.
Give thanks to God, you cricket lovers,
for food and drink. Remove the covers!

*A grace written to mark a birthday celebration in honour of the
late Brian Johnstone's 80th birthday*

Patrick Forbes

Girl Guides

For food in a world where many
   walk in hunger,
For faith in a world where many
   walk in fear,
For friends in a world where many
   walk alone,
We give you humble thanks, O Lord.

'World Hunger Grace' Girl Guides of Canada

The Scouts

For food, for clothing, for friendship
   for scouting,
Lord we thank you.

Humorous graces

For every cup and plateful,
May the Lord God make us grateful.

God bless this bunch as they munch
    their lunch.

I'm ready for it, Lord,
and it's ready for me!

For porridge and for buttered toast
Praise Father, Son and Holy Ghost.

H. Ingamells

✳

This is the day the Lord has made
Thank you for the toast and marmalade.

✳

For cabbage, corn and shepherd's pie.
We praise the Lord who dwells on high.

H. Ingamells

✳

For well-filled plate
And brimming cup
And freedom from the washing up.
We thank you, Lord. Amen.

Lord, as we begin this new day,
Help us not to be like porridge,
Stiff and stodgy and slow to stir,
But like cornflakes,
Crisp and light and ready to serve.

Lord, as we begin this new day,
Help us not to be like cornflakes,
Lightweight, brittle and cold,
But like porridge,
Warm, comforting and full of goodness.

Plaice, mackerel, haddock and cod,
these are the fish we eat, O God.
For prawns and shrimps, sardines on toast,
praise Father, Son and Holy Ghost.

Christopher Herbert

Thanks for breakfast, lunch and dinner,
If it weren't for you I'd be much thinner.

For bread and wine
And Auld Lang Syne,
God's holy name be praised.

Rub-a-dub-dub,
Thanks for the grub.

*

Thanks for chickens, thanks for eggs,
But why so many chicken legs ... ?
For custard creams and apple crumble,
Just bless the Lord and don't you grumble.

*

HISTORICAL GRACES

Lord Christ, we pray thy mercy on our
    table spread,
And what thy gentle hands have given
    thy men
Let it by thee be blessed.
Whatever we have came from thy lavish
    heart and gentle hand,
And all that's good is thine, for thou
    art good.
And ye that eat, give thanks for it to Christ,
And let the words ye utter be only peace,
For Christ loved peace. It was himself
    that said,
Peace I give unto you, my peace I leave
    with you.
Grant that your own may be a generous hand
Breaking the bread for all poor men,
    sharing the food.
Christ shall receive the bread thou gavest
    his poor,
And shall not tarry to give thee reward.

Alcuin of York (735–804)

To God who gives our daily bread
A thankful song we raise,
And pray that he who sends us food
ay fill our hearts with praise.

Thomas Tallis (c.1510–85)

The eyes of all things do look up and trust
in Thee; O Lord, thou givest them their
meat in due season. Thou dost open thy
hand and fillest with thy blessing
everything living. Good Lord, bless us
and all thy goods which we receive of
thy bountiful liberality:
Through Jesus Christ our Lord.

Queen Elizabeth I (1533–1603)

Thou that givest food to all flesh
which feed'st the young ravens that cry
   unto thee
and hast nourished us from our youth up:
Fill our hearts with good and gladness
and establish our hearts with thy grace.

Lancelot Andrewes (1555–1626)

What God gives, and what we take,
'tis a gift for Christ his sake.
Be the meal of beans and peas,
God be thanked for those and these,
Have we flesh or have we fish,
All are fragments from his dish.
He his Church save, and the king,
and our peace here, like a spring,
make it ever flourishing.

Robert Herrick (1591–1674)

God! To my little meal and oil
Add but a bit of flesh to boil
And thou my pipkinnet shalt see
Give a wave-offering to thee.

Robert Herrick (1591–1674)

Thou who has given so much to me
Give one thing more, a grateful heart,
for Christ's sake.

George Herbert (1593–1632)

Most gracious God, who has given us
Christ and with him all that is necessary to
life and godliness: we thankfully take this
our food as the gift of thy bounty, procured
by his merits. Bless it to the nourishment
and strength of our frail bodies to fit us
for thy cheerful service.

Richard Baxter (1615–91)

God send this crumb well down.

Prayer of a Royalist during the English Civil War

Lord, grant that whether I eat or drink,
or whatever I do, I may do all to thy glory.

Thomas Ken (1637–1711)

Bless me, O Lord, and let my food
strengthen me to serve thee,
for Jesus Christ's sake.

Isaac Watts (1674–1748)

Be present at our table, Lord,
Be here and everywhere adored
Thy creatures bless and grant that we
May feast in paradise with thee.

John Wesley (1703–92)

Thy providence supplies my food
And 'tis thy blessing makes it good.
My soul is nourished by thy word.
Let soul and body praise the Lord.

William Cowper (1731–1800)

For life and love, for rest and food,
For daily help and nightly care
Sing to the Lord for he is good,
And praise his name for it is fair.

J. S. B. Monsell (1811–75)

And when thou art at thy meat, praise thy God:
In thought at ilke morsel and say thus in
thy heart:
Loved be thou king and thanked be thou king
and blessed be thou king.
Ihesu all my joying of all thy giftes good
that for me spilt thy blood and died on
the rood.
Thou gave me grace to sing
the song of thy loving
my praise to thee ay spring
withouten any feigning.

The Lay Folks' Mass Book

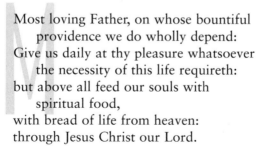

Most loving Father, on whose bountiful
providence we do wholly depend:
Give us daily at thy pleasure whatsoever
the necessity of this life requireth:
but above all feed our souls with
spiritual food,
with bread of life from heaven:
through Jesus Christ our Lord.

From Christian Prayers 1578 (after Erasmus)

GRACES FOR CHILDREN

Bread is a lovely thing to eat –
God bless the barley and the wheat;
A lovely thing to breathe is air –
God bless the sunshine everywhere;
The earth's a lovely place to know –
God bless the folks that come and go!
Alive's a lovely thing to be,
Giver of life – we say – bless thee!

For birds and beasts and bugs and bees,
For fields and flowers and weeds and trees,
For schools and teachers, girls and boys,
Families, friends and crazy toys,
For love and laughter, food and fun,
We thank you, God, for every one.

Patrick Forbes

Here a little child I stand,
Heaving up my either hand:
Cold as paddocks though they be,
Here I lift them up to Thee,
For a benison to fall
On our meat and on our all. Amen.

Robert Herrick (1591–1674)
('paddocks' are toads; a 'benison' is a blessing)

*

Our Father God, in whom we live,
Accept the thanks thy children give,
Our needs are by thy bounty met,
May we the giver ne'er forget.

Robert Walmsley (1831–1905)

*

For water-ices, cheap but good,
that find us in a thirsty mood;
for ices made of milk or cream
that slip down smoothly as a dream;
for cornets, sandwiches and pies
that make the gastric juices rise;
for ices bought in little shops
or at the kerb from him who stops;
for chanting of the sweet refrain:
'chocolate, strawberry or plain?'
We thank thee, Lord, who sends with
      the heat
this cool deliciousness to eat.

Christopher Herbert

GRACES BY CHILDREN

God is great, God is good,
Thank you, Lord, for all our food.

Traditional German children's grace

Dear Lord Jesus, I'm sorry.
Sometimes I think about food too much.
I dream of all the delicious things there are
    to eat when I really should be doing
    other things.
Please help me not to make food so
    important, and help me not to be
    greedy at meal times. Amen.

For my daily food, I thank you, Lord,
For the farmers, shopkeepers and cooks
    who prepare my food,
        I thank you, Lord.
For my favourite foods, I thank you, Lord.
Help us to care about people not having
        enough food. Amen

Thank you, Lord, for the food we eat,
for the clothes we wear,
for the games we play.
Help us never to forget those who have
little food to eat
and few clothes to wear,
and no strength for playing games.

Lord, bless this food and our family.

Nigel Nyumbu (aged 12)

＊

Thank you, Lord, for this lovely food.

Miranda Nyumbu (aged 4)

＊

God, thank you for the food we eat each day and help all the people around the world with nothing but your love.

Ravitta Jisdhaul (aged 11)

＊

My prayer of thanksgiving for the food
   we eat, Amen, Amen.
For the friends we have, Amen, Amen.
For the love you give us. Amen, Amen.

Michael Baird (aged 9)

Dear God, thank you for food,
So we can be in a good mood,
And thank you for friends and family,
So we can all live happily. Amen

Jessica Mistry (aged 10)

Dear God,
Thank you for the food you provide
   us with.
Bless all the animals who give us meat
and farmers who grow vegetables
so we have plenty to eat. Amen.

Kelly Devane (aged 10)

Thank you for our food,
Thank you for shops that sell us food.
Thank you for the water from the sky.
Thank you for being God. Amen

Charlotte Franklin (aged 8)

Thank you for food and kindness,
Thank you for warmth and friends.
Thank you for trees and plants
And everything that gives us life. Amen.

Lee Simms (aged 7)

Dear God,
Thank you for our food that we eat
    and for drinks.
Please help all the other children and
    parents to keep alive. Amen.

Hayley Reeves (aged 7)

Dear God,
Thank you for our food that makes us
      healthy and for the water that we drink
      and thank you for giving us a family.
We are lucky to have a Mum and we are
      lucky to have a God like you.

Dipesh Mistry (aged 7)

✳

Dear God,
Thank you for my home
      and the rain and sun.
Thank you for my toys and food and fun.
Thank you for my school and all your gifts
      to me.
Thank you God for your generosity.

✳

My dear loving God,
This prayer is to thank you for this special
    world that I have been living in.
Thank you for your kindness and all your
    gifts to us.
Thank you for our food and please help us
    to think about other people
    who are hungry. Amen.

Tanya Walker (aged 8)

✳

Dear God,
Thank you for food and drink,
Thank you for the way we think,
Thank you for flesh and meat,
Thank you for our arms and feet. Amen.

Nilesh Mistry (aged 8)

✳

Dear God,
Thank you for giving us food, water, life
    and animals.
Thank you for being our God,
Thank you for helping us. Amen.

Harinder Kaur (aged 9)

Dear Lord,
Thank you for our food and bless
    the hands that make the food.
Bless us, O Lord, and thanks for all
    my friends and my Mom and Dad.

Adam King (aged 5)

Dear Father God,
We thank you for our food and drink.
Thank you for sending the rain and the sun
to make the corn grow so that the baker
can make our bread and cakes.
Amen.

Anna Bennett (aged 6)

Dear Father God,
Thank you for the food we eat
    especially the chips and hot dogs.
Thank you for the hot dog man
    who makes them for me. Amen.

Ajay Jilka (aged 6)

Dear God,
Thank you for the cheese and peanut butter
   and jam for my sandwiches.

Adam Martin (aged 5)

Thank you, God, for all our food.
Thank you for keeping the fishermen safe
   when they are at sea catching fish
   for my dinner.
Amen.

Henry Miller (aged 6)

Dear Father God,
Thank you for my Mummy who cleans my
   bedroom and cooks my tea. Amen.

James Marlow (aged 5)

Thank you, God, for our food and drink
and our toys.
Thank you, God, for my friends who play
with me.
Thank you for my Mummy and Daddy.
Amen.

Christopher Halliwell (aged 6)

GRACES FROM AROUND THE WORLD

Scotland

Some hae meat and canna eat.
And some wad eat that want it.
But we hae meat and we can eat
Ans sae the Lord be thankit.

Selkirk Grace
Robert Burns (1759–96)

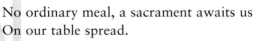

No ordinary meal, a sacrament awaits us
On our table spread.
For men are risking lives on sea and land
That we may dwell in safety and be fed.

Doon head
Up paws
Thank God
We've jaws.

Wales

O Arglwdd bendithia'n bwyd, i'n cadw'n
    fyw i'th wasanaethu Di,
drwy Iesu Grist. Amen.

O Lord, bless our food, that keeps us alive
    to serve thee,
through Jesus Christ our Lord. Amen.

John Parry

Africa

God of my needfulness,
grant me something to eat,
give me milk, give me sons,
give me herds, give me meat, O my Father.

African morning invocation

The bread is pure and fresh,
The water cool and clear.
Lord of all life be with us,
Lord of all life be near.

O Lord, our meal is steaming before us and it smells very good. The water is clear and fresh. We are happy and satisfied. But now we think of our sisters and brothers all over the world who have nothing to eat and only a little to drink. Please, please through the help of their sisters and brothers, let them have enough to eat and enough to drink.

Prayer from West Africa

Brazil

My God, I thank you for my food. It is you that allows the rice, the beans, the wheat, the fruit, the animals and the vegetables to grow. Thank you for the food that is on the table. Thank you very much.

Elizite Simon (aged 11)

China

Each time we eat, may we remember
God's love.

*

Egypt

O Lord, who fed the multitudes with
five barley loaves, bless what we
are about to eat.

*

Germany

Come, Lord Jesus, be our guest,
and may our meal by you be blest.

Traditional German grace attributed to
Martin Luther (1483–1546)

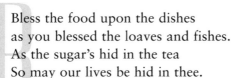

Bless the food upon the dishes
as you blessed the loaves and fishes.
As the sugar's hid in the tea
So may our lives be hid in thee.

Hawaii

Bless our home, Father,
that we cherish the bread before there
   is none,
discover each other before we leave,
and enjoy each other for what we are,
   while we have time.

India

For sharing your spirit with the whole
household of faith, that it may become
your new extended family with always
room for more around the table.
We thank you, good Father of us all.
Amen. So be it.

Litany of thanksgiving for homes used in Andrha Pradesh

O God above,
Make good for us all that we
     have cultivated.
Let it bear good fruit!
Let it be good fruit for us.
We shall eat new fruits.
Green mangoes, ripe mangoes,
     mophua, dates,
Let them be for our whole well being.
Deliver us from the tiger, the bear,
     the snake,
From all these venomous beasts:
Deliver us from all manner of disease
From suffering unto death,
And from all our enemies.

*Invocation used at the community eating of the first-fruits
among the tribal people of the Kond Hills in India*

*

Switzerland

Because you are the Creator
and provider of everything,
Father God, as trusting children
do we pray to you
for our daily bread.

Strasbourg Hymnal

Praised be your loyalty,
You Father of all grace,
which today has blessed
us richly once again.

You give us at all times
here on earth our daily bread.
O bless us with peace
In life and in death.

R. Wimmer

You present us, God, so fatherly
now food and drink: we praise you,
because everything which nourishes and
strengthens us, is given by your hand.

Sixteenth-century prayer printed on a serviette in a Swiss hotel

With every bite we eat
We do not want to forget to give thanks.
Whatever brings us your blessing shall be
    to the glory of your name.
Give thanks to the Lord because he is kind
    and his goodness will last forever.
Now let us give to God the Lord thanks,
    and give him glory for all his gifts
    which we have received.

Ludwig Helmbold (1532–98)

United States of America

God of grace,
sustain our bodies with this food,
our hearts with true friendship
and our souls with your truth,
for Christ's sake.
Amen.

Lord Jesus, be our holy guest,
our morning joy, our evening rest;
and with our daily bread impart
your love and peace to every heart.
Amen.

Blessed are you, Lord.
You have fed us from the earliest days.
You give food to every living creature.
Fill our hearts with joy and delight.
Let us always have enough and something
    to spare for works of mercy
In honour of Christ Jesus, our Lord.

Through him may glory, honour and power
    be yours forever. Amen.

The eyes of all wait upon you, O Lord,
And you give them their food in due season.
You open your hand
And fill all living things with plenteousness.
Amen.

GRACES FOR SPECIAL OCCASIONS

Weddings

For the joys of meeting, greeting
    and eating.
We give you thanks.

Bishop Gavin Reid

For all this day's reminders
That you are a God of love.
We give you thanks. Amen.

Bishop Gavin Reid

Heavenly Father, God of love, thank you
for the gift of marriage which we
celebrate today.
Thank you for this marvellous wedding
feast spread before us and for the
friends and family gathered here
to share it.
Bless us now as we eat, and particularly
bless (*John and Mary*) in their new
life together. May every meal time
be as happy for them as this.
Amen.

Helena Smalman-Smith

Harvest

We thank thee now, O Father
For all things bright and good
The seed time and the harvest
Our life, our health, our food.
No gifts have we to offer
For all thy love imparts
But that which thou desirest
Our humble, grateful hearts.

All good gifts around us
Are sent from heaven above.
Then thank the Lord,
O thank the Lord
For all his love.

Matthias Claudius (1740–1815)

We dare not ask you bless our harvest feast
'til it is spread for poorest and for least,
We dare not bring our harvest gifts to you
Unless our hungry brothers share them too.

Not only at this time, Lord, every day
Those whom you love are dying
    while we pray,
Teach us to do with less, and so to share
From our abundance more than we
    can spare.

Now with this harvest plenty round
    us piled,
Show us the Christ in every starving child;
Speak, as you spoke of old in Galilee,
'You feed, or you refuse, not them but me'.

Lilian Cox

✳

Birthdays

For friends and presents,
Birthday cake and candles,
Balloons and parties and friends
    to share them all,
A year gone by and a new year
    to look forward to,
we thank you, Lord.

Helena Smalman-Smith

Picnics

For the sandwiches, fruit, crisps and cakes
Spread out here upon the grass (*or sand*),
Even for the insects which want
    to share it with us,
We thank you, Lord.
It is a privilege to eat your gifts
    of fresh food here
In the fresh air of your creation.

Helena Smalman-Smith

Lent

Instead of living it up
Try giving it up ... for Lent.
Chocolates, sweets, a glass of beer,
Swearing, eating to excess ...
And then spend what you save to bless
The poor.
Give thanks to God for all he gives,
For Christ, once dead, now lives!

Patrick Forbes

Easter

On this Easter day we thank you that you
gave your life to save us from our sin,
We thank you that you rose from the dead
to give us life,
and we thank you that each new day you
give us our daily bread.

Pam Robertson

The yeast in the hot cross buns transforms
the dough and makes them rise.
Lord, whenever we see these familiar
symbols of your glorious resurrection
during this season of Eastertide, help us
to remember how you transformed the
world by rising victorious on Easter day.
Amen.

Helena Smalman-Smith

Christmas

Thank you for our food this day and
thank you for the reminder that Christ
the Saviour of mankind is born. Amen.

For holly's cheerful crimson berry,
For children's faces shining merry,
For all our loved ones gathered here,
For absent loved ones far and near,
For food to hearten us in eating,
For wine to gladden us in drinking,
For love, for health, for happiness,
For joy and faith and hope of peace,
For countless other gifts beside,
We thank thee, Lord, this Christmastide.

A Women's Institute Christmas grace

MUSICAL GRACES

Praise God from whom all blessings flow,
Praise Him all creatures here below,
Praise Him above the heavenly host.
Praise Father, Son and Holy Ghost.

Thomas Ken (1637–1711)

Praise God from whom all bless- ings flow, Praise
Him all crea- tures here be- low. Praise
Him a- bove the hea- ven- ly host, Praise
Fa- ther Son and Ho- ly Ghost.

We thank you, Lord, for daily food,
and every other thing that's good:
music and art and friends to share
the gift of life in every mood.

But who can handle every mood,
save he who gives us daily food,
the Lord who hears and answers prayer,
and holds us firm for all that's good?

So, Lord, we praise you, wholly good,
and seek your help in every mood
to show our neighbours proper care,
and share with all our daily food.

Jock Stein

Here is our food and we'll share it out
    among us all,
Gathered from north, south, west and east;
And we'll sing as we eat with Jesus in
    our company,
'Who'll come and share
    in the kingdom feast?'

We're on a journey, we're on a journey,
We're on a journey, a faith pilgrimage,
And we'll sing as we eat with Jesus in
    our company,
'Who'll come and share
    in the kingdom feast?'

Jock Stein

The Lord is good to me,
And so I thank the Lord
For giving me the things I need
The sun, the rain and the appleseed.
The Lord is good to me.

And every seed that grows
Will grow into a tree.
And one day soon
There'll be apples there,
For everyone in the world to share,
The Lord is good to me.

'Johnny Appleseed grace'
John Chapman (1774–1845)

Thank you for the world so sweet,
Thank you for the food we eat,
Thank you for the birds that sing,
Thank you, God, for everything.

E. Rutter Leatham

Thank you for the world so sweet, Thank you for the food we eat,

Thank you for the birds that sing, Thank you, God, for ev-ery-thing.

For health and strength and daily food,
we praise your name, O God.

May be sung as a 4-part round

For health and strength and dai- ly food we

praise your name O God.

LATIN GRACES

Dominus Jesus, sit potus et esus.

Lord Jesus, be drink and food.

Martin Luther (1483–1546)

Benedic, Domine, nobis et his donis tuis,
quae tua gratia et munificentia sumus iam
sumpturi; et concede ut illis salubriter a te
nutriti tibi debitum obsequium praestare
valeamus per Christum Dominum nostrum.
Amen.

Lord, bless us and these thy gifts which
with thy grace and bounty we are now to
eat; and grant that, nourished therewith by
thee to our health, we may honour thee
with the praise which we owe thee, through
Christ our Lord. Amen.

King's College, Cambridge

INDEX OF FIRST LINES

INDEX OF AUTHORS AND SOURCES

INDEX OF OCCASIONS AND SUBJECTS

ACKNOWLEDGEMENTS

The compiler and publisher gratefully
acknowledge permission to reproduce copyright
material in this anthology. Every effort has been
made to trace and contact copyright holders.
If there are any inadvertent omissions we
apologize to those concerned and will ensure
that a suitable acknowlegement is made at the
next reprint.

Scripture quotations taken from the Holy Bible,
New International Version © 1973, 1978,
1984 by International Bible Society. Used by
permission of Hodder & Stoughton Ltd.
All rights reserved.

Curtis Brown: from Campling and Davis (eds),
Words for Worship (pp. 8, 9).
The Continuum Publishing Group: from *The
Prayer Manual* (p. 10) and from David Silk (ed.),
Prayers for Use at the Alternative Services (p. 7).
The Reverend Patrick Forbes (pp. 16, 19, 33, 64).
The Girl Guides of Canada: the Hunger Task
Force, *World Hunger Grace*. Anglican Church
Diocese of Huron (p. 20).
HarperCollins Publishers Ltd: from Giles and
Melville Harcourt (compilers), *Short Prayers*

for the Long Day (p. 8) and from Elizabeth
Laird, *Prayers for Children* (p. 37).
The Right Reverend Christopher Herbert
(pp. 17, 18, 24, 35).
Hodder & Stoughton: from Tony Castle (ed.),
A Treasury of Prayer (p. 7) and Janet Lynch-
Watson, *A Patchwork Prayer* (p. 36).
The Reverend H. Ingamells (p. 22).
Kingsway Publications: from Dick Williams
(ed.), *Prayers for Today's Church* © 1972 (p. 5).
David W. Lankshear (p. 4).
Lion Publishing: from *365 Children's Prayers*
(p. 38).
The Liturgical Press, Collegeville, Minnesota:
from Stephen Doyle, *The Pilgrim's Guide to the
Holy Land* © 1985 The Order of St Benedict,
Inc. (p. 9).
The Lutheran World Federation (p. 51).
Oxford University Press: from George Appleton
(ed.), *The Oxford Book of Prayer* (p. 7).
Bishop Gavin Reid (p. 59).
Pam Robertson (pp. 3, 64).
The Scout Association, London: from *Scout
Prayers* (p. 20).
Helena Smalman-Smith (pp. 60, 63, 65).
SPCK: from J. Carden (compiler), *Another Day*,
(pp. 50, 53) and Lilian Cox, *A Little Book of
Prayers* (p. 62).
Audrey Stanley (p. 4).

Jock Stein (pp. 68, 70).
United Nations Music Publishing: for a tune
© 1972 Jimmy Owen (p. 67).
The Westminster Press, Philadelphia, from
Daily Prayer: The Worship of God (pp. 57, 58).